# WORD

# BY

# WORD

---

Poems Inspired by Scripture

PIERCE TAYLOR HIBBS

Scripture quotations are from the ESV® Bible (The Holy Bible, English Standard Version®), copyright © 2001 by Crossway, a publishing ministry of Good News Publishers. Used by permission. All rights reserved.

Paperback ISBN: 979-8-9861067-4-8

## Other Books by the Author

*In Divine Company*
*Theological English*
*The Trinity, Language, and Human Behavior*
*The Speaking Trinity & His Worded World*
*Finding God in the Ordinary*
*Struck Down but Not Destroyed*
*Sill, Silent, and Strong*
*Finding Hope in Hard Things*
*The Book of Giving*
*I Am a Human*
*The Great Lie*
*God of Words*
*Christmas Glory*

## Other Poetry Collections

*Borrowed Images: Prose Poems*

# Contents

### *The Gathering*

Prayers were once
quiet conversation
with man and God,
not the ladder
we wait at the bottom of.

Adam and Eve,
they loved talk purely.
The words made each day
a gathering,
and God the soft 'yes'
filling in the spaces
between every naked
silence.

## Offerings

Cain gathered from the earth
proud red tomatoes, carrots
orange as the setting sun,
grapes hanging from green threads,
purple—a color they could not imagine.
But he brought less than he could.

The other gathered the life
stored in fat around the kidneys
and the hind legs.
Paradise was gone but for fat.

He found the lamb walking the fields at dawn,
opened up its heart,
found YHWH in the blood,
and wept.

Paradise Abel brought before God,
burned the fat with flame,
bowed down and begged,
offering himself as much as the lamb.

What more can we do?

### *Abraham (Gen 12:1)*

> "Now the LORD said to Abram, 'Go from
> your country and your kindred and your
> father's house to the land that I will show
> you.'"

There now, traveler.
You are an enigma in your father's house.

Walk with me;
with me walk through the wild,
through slave fields,
through the sea.

Your greatest grandchildren
I will teach to fish.
And their fishing will evaporate them
as they burn white as stars.
I will pull from your body
a long line
that loves
to place one foot
on top of the other,
arms out,
chasing eternity.

### Ichthus

Down through the water he came and swam.
I am. I am. I am.

He found the atmosphere
dark and diseased.
Our fins were thin and tight,
our hope held together
with muscle and bone.
Even this weak,
we still set out our possessions
on sandbars,
swimming the perimeter
to protect them, as seals.

But *I am* gathered no things.
*I am* brought the gift of light
down to the water,
that by his scales
he might redeem the dark.

With his fish body,
baptized in sorrow,
he laid himself upon a plank of wood,
calling all schools together.
He was lifted up, above the waters.

And then down to the water he went,
shuffling his fins in the deep.

We thought he was spent,
but he was only asleep.

### Suffering Unto Glory

When I ask for peace in your name,
do I ask to be crucified?
Do I ask for thorns?
Do I call out the crowds as birds
And invite their hackling?
Do I ready my neck to drop
because "it is finished"?

But if these things I can imagine,
why not the white peace that adored you?
Why not your Father's face
as he lifted you up like a small fish from a dark
puddle?
Why not your arms,
spread as wings on a cross?
Why not *my* arms,
opened wide as a pigeon's
over the city.
Why do I not take the time
to feel the sunlight on my face,
as I emerge from my snakeskin tomb,
resurrected,
born of Spirit?

### The Antidote

Poison, as fire, follows open spaces.
Contamination is a weed we cannot help
but call ugly. It hurts. It grows.
It hurts more. It whispers death
And that sounds like 'ending'.

We beg for reversal, the antidote,
for something to go where the poison went,
to turn the cells of poison in on themselves,
dividing kingdoms.

And so the antidote surrenders
having already won.
It renews the inside
to restore the outside.

## The Ripping (Mark 1:10; 14:63; 15:38)

> "And when he came up out of the water, immediately he saw the heavens being torn open and the Spirit descending on him like a dove" (Mark 1:10).
> "And the high priest tore his garments and said, 'What further witnesses do we need?'" (Mark 14:63)
> "And the curtain of the temple was torn in two, from top to bottom" (Mark 15:38).

Torn the sky.
Torn the garments.
Torn the thick veil.

The Messiah is a ripper.
Sky over water,
cloth over heart,
cloth over holy.

Painful? Yes.
Only because of the brightness,
because of the honesty,
because of the channel
too wide now to deny.

It's the ripping that makes a river.

"There is a river whose channel
makes glad the city of God."

## *John 1:1*

> "In the beginning was the Word, and the Word
> was with God, and the Word was God."

I hunt the word.
I hunt he that wants to be hunted.
And his resurrection echoes.

His falling and rising

is the hoof
is the beat
is the hoof
is the beat

that leads to mine.

### *Revelation 21:4*

> "He will wipe away every tear from their eyes,
> and death shall be no more, neither shall there
> be mourning, nor crying, nor pain anymore,
> for the former things have passed away."

Gone the hair that falls, as grass, from cancer.
Gone the fear of death that has no answer.
Gone the sea and thunder of the deep.
Gone the cycle of birth, death, and weep.

Gone confusing are the words we speak.
We are a shadow of the hope we keep.
But gone the sun that draws a shadow out.
Gone the shadows and the temple mount.

### *Genesis 3:9*

> "But the LORD God called to the man and
> said to him, 'Where are you?'"

Unless spoken to
we all wither away.
It's dialogue or death.

I say: Speak to me Moore.
Call me out of cave.
The light, it matters,
but I want to hear.

Sound saves.
The crucifixion is invisible,
but the hammer and steel,
the yawning wood,
the desperation of no *and* yes…

I take salvation by the first letter,
go syllable by syllable
to the n.

### Matthew 6:22–23

> "The eye is the lamp of the body. So, if your
> eye is healthy, your whole body will be full of
> light, but if your eye is bad, your whole body
> will be full of darkness. If then the light in you
> is darkness, how great is the darkness!"

It is windy.
The bones of the house are playing sour
violins,
Wind is heavy like thunder outside,
But I am within.
It is my silence that allows the sound,
My quiet blood hearing, hearing, hearing
And hating the salt of sight.
This is how I ignore everything unimportant:
I open my eyes loud.

## *Job 1:21*

> And he said, "Naked I came from my mother's
> womb, and naked shall I return. The LORD
> gave, and the LORD has taken away; blessed
> be the name of the LORD."

It was the cold that brought me in.
I did not need gloves; I had my skin.

And when I go out, it will be the cold
that ushers me out,
but not in skin.
The dark recognizes no such thing,
and the light would breathe it right in.

### A Confession

I let it go
down from my hands.
They were closed
but the light asked so quietly
that I let him through the cracks.
I took my compressed kingdom,
opened one gate at a time,
finger by finger war heroes
laying down sword and shield,
selling back land stolen
between sunset and sunrise,
shivering into the surrender.

I had every chance to re-arm
and go white bone again
but
decided against it.
I let the stone go.
I like to have my pockets clean
and hands open as sails.

### The Fall

We had seen some fire in the distance,
from up in the canopy of innocence.
Looking at one another staring at the flame,
we knew then we could be burned.
Our skin wrapped the life blood that would
ignite
even with His whisper.

We stopped listening to the flame when the
other creatures came.
One by one, our stems broke off at the root,
color left with descent.
At the garden floor, we were now scared of
being burned.
Out of the canopy, flame could fly right into
our veins;
such combustion, we would learn,
is the only way to elevate.

### *Matthew 27:50*

> "And Jesus cried out again with a loud voice
> and yielded up his spirit."

He gave so
oh much for stranger souls
to believe.

Blood is heavy
and screams "stop,"
but oh
no: let it be.

### Exodus

I begin borrowing,
borrowing to begin.

And once I'm in,
I feel I own down to the bone.
Exodus is offering back
what should not have been taken,
not taking
what is offered.

### The Stars (Nehemiah 4:21)

> "So we labored at the work, and half of them
> held the spears from the break of dawn until
> the stars came out."

How can you be content to burn
for your whole life
and only be seen for half of it?
Breadcrumbs from God's table
are a reminder:
it is what we do at night
that matters most.

### *Flood-beat (Genesis 6–9)*

The flood was a heartbeat to God.
Down came the rain;
in came the people,
contracted to a wooden hull.

And the heart stayed closed
for forty days, forty nights.
Months later the sun rose;
the boat broke open.
Noah shipwrecked on life
and began, a fearful wooden heart,
to expand again.

### *The Eyes and the Heartbeat (Gen 6:8)*

> "But Noah found favor in the eyes of
> the Lord."

I have made my contract
with Him invisible;
with Him I am tightly bound channels,
routes rushing together,
blood mingled.

I don't expect to expand.
Freedom is weighed out in breaths,
while death is cat-quiet in the bushes.
With Him my channels open,
and out of joy
I stare at myself,
only to contract,
as Job on the dusty earth,
awaiting rebirth
in the weightless heart of God.

### *Hebrews 4:15*

> "For we do not have a high priest who is
> unable to sympathize with our weaknesses, but
> one who in every respect has been tempted as
> we are, yet without sin."

Holy painter,
covered in color,
dripping with residue,
tracking tempura,
I want to be touched.

Never much for isolation;
never much for loneliness.
Let us talk, you and I.
Let us borrow colors.

### *John 8:6–8*

> "This they said to test him, that they might
> have some charge to bring against him. Jesus
> bent down and wrote with his finger on the
> ground. And as they continued to ask him,
> he stood up and said to them, 'Let him who
> is without sin among you be the first to throw
> a stone at her.' And once more he bent down
> and wrote on the ground."

Draw, my Word. Draw in the dust
words too great for reed and paper,
words no one will read, my maker.

I draw sounds with my hands
while you drew life into dirt.
All of my words drown out
in the water of doubt.
You, speaker, breathe on the water,
separate one thing from another,
draw each detail.
When our feet have erased them,
we depend on your memory.

## *Matthew 27:45–46*

> "Now from the sixth hour there was darkness
> over all the land until the ninth hour. And
> about the ninth hour Jesus cried out with a
> loud voice, saying, 'Eli, Eli, lema sabachthani?'
> that is, 'My God, my God, why have you
> forsaken me?'"

The heat of his tears,
warm salt of sadness,
the valley, nose and cheekbone . . .
What is left to do
when it's already been decided
but to bow your head
and trust in the love
watching from beyond the sun?

### *Psalm 127:1–2*

Unless the Lord builds the house,
    those who build it labor in vain.
Unless the Lord watches over the city,
    the watchman stays awake in vain.
It is in vain that you rise up early
    and go late to rest,
eating the bread of anxious toil;
    for he gives to his beloved sleep.

I thought the hammer strike was mine
and the leather pouch, covered in paint,
holding nails that fingers pick a fight with.
The nails too; what is a hammer
without something to hit?

If they are not mine,
what love has spent my life
white-knuckling every carpenter's tool,
holding the wood and metal in place,
raising up the framework
in silence?

### The Bible

Gather the sheep skins
and the goat hides;
gather the shoulder blades of camels;
turn the animals outside in;
we've used them already once for sin.
Map the epidermis with where we've been.
Sign each skin in blood.
The Spirit will show each
the road between the front
and back cover
that we might love one another
as paragraphs in one story,
bleeding out and breathing glory.

### Rolled Away

The stone was heavy.
My life is weak.
Behind it lie some broken bones.
For now, I am frustrated by linen,
the way it hems me in.

But how quickening will be
the sliver of light on me
when the door of time opens wide
and a deafening wind calls me inside.

### Lazarus's Sister

Death is a closed door, master;
let me in.
Death is a closed door, master;
let me in.

He went away without me
and now my eyes are swollen.
The whole earth stretches light
from my tears, because our years
have ended half ended.

Christ:
The latch is open, woman;
the door is no secret thing.
Lazarus, sweet Lazarus,
next of kin, cold and thin,
will warm under the Son
and flower before us here,
even though spring is
a whisper in the wind.

A voice is coming
to deafen death.

### Psalm 91

God, my great bird.
The sky is free as breath to you,
and the earth a post for your talons.
Yet, here I sit beside them,
so sure that the smooth, hard surface
is just another rock.

My home is cast of shadow,
and I play in the canopy of your quills.
I thought you were a song bird.
I thought you turned out music,
but music, it turns out, is in a word,
a thing understood and unspoken.

## *Genesis 1:4*

> "And God saw that the light was good. And
> God separated the light from the darkness."

The dog turns over under the table,
pushes his body into the sun.
Someone left the white blinds open.

The sliding glass door stood before God,
covered in the cloud of dog snout
and children's finger smears.
Light came in un-damned
and said, "I am here."
The dog responds to its gesture,
and as the dust and hair roll into the open,
says likewise, "this is good."

### The Prologue

Christ came to my ear,
came through a dark tomb,
rolled my soul around
as a stone.

Sound goes to the bone.
It moves the marrow,
then waits contently,
as a bird on a wire,
ready to teach flight.

## *2 Corinthians 12:10*

> "For the sake of Christ, then, I am content
> with weaknesses, insults, hardships,
> persecutions, and calamities. For when I am
> weak, then I am strong."

I don't remember my victories.
What is it to stand on a hill?

In the valley of deep shadow,
thrones are being built
of alabaster and marble.
These are invisible in the dark.
But the flutter of bird wings,
dealings with the wind,
these I can *see*;
these I trust.

As I come up from the dust,
claw to the hilltop,
I see the kingdom assembled
and my doubt running as a river,
running as a river behind me.

### *Luke 6:20*

> "And he lifted up his eyes on his disciples, and
> said: 'Blessed are you who are poor, for yours is
> the kingdom of God.'"

Blessed are the poor,
those who are wanting,
those who are waiting
with empty metal cups
for change.

This side of paradise is what we know;
the high and the low,
the deep and the shallow,
the poor and those who want more.
This side of paradise is a mirror.

### The Name

Shakespeare was wrong;
there *is* something in a name.
Our names are echoes.
A thing speaks; we speak back.
But our naming is shy and shallow,
puddles on a thin dirt road.
Our names make sense because of the rain.

Not like the river,
not like the name that causes the echo,
not like the voice that breathes from beneath
the earth,
calls to son and daughter,
makes resurrection out of water.

### *James 1:2*

> "Count it all joy, my brothers, when you meet
> trials of various kinds."

The joy is one thing.
In your hand it is raw,
unformed, and quiet.
James was working on shape,
burnishing himself away
like a man happy with tools,
who then becomes one of them
and works so well.

### *Psalm 143:6*

> "I stretch out my hands to you;
> my soul thirsts for you like a parched land."

The water is running out.
Our field has been flooded,
the summer blood spent
pushing out the pollen,
and the first flowers have risen
and fallen, swollen with pride.
This is how Christ died,
but came back in a river
no man or devil
could ever damn.

### Revelation 19:21

> "And the rest were slain by the sword that
> came from the mouth of him who was sitting
> on the horse, and all the birds were gorged
> with their flesh."

The birds were fat and heavy,
consuming the diminished,
turning death to life
in small stomachs,
flying off with bodies
full of what is right
taken from what is wrong.

### Revelation 20:10

> "And the devil who had deceived them was
> thrown into the lake of fire and sulfur where
> the beast and the false prophet were, and they
> will be tormented day and night forever and
> ever."

When deception is burned away,
as spider webbing in a barn corner,
then the room will become free and open;
the walls may even fall away,
leaving us not to ourselves
but to the one who speaks things
as they are.

### *Listen*

Eden came of sound;
out from the dark of God's mouth
came the sound of the river trout,
the soft applause of grass,
the orca sonar, sounding in the deep.

The crescendo rolled in like a wave
bubbling and settling, one word on another.

When our eyes had opened,
diminuendo danced in;
someone's voice echoed out,
and we found speech
in pools of water in the leaves.

## *Agree and Return (Job 22:21–23)*

"Agree with God, and be at peace;
    thereby good will come to you.
Receive instruction from his mouth,
    and lay up his words in your heart.
If you return to the Almighty you will be built up;
    if you remove injustice far from your tents."

Light flooded over the hillside
before I was aware.
I arose a man of cloth,
looking for a breeze
and found it like lost sheet music
slipping through the trees.

I am frustrated.
The storm-brought dirt
covering my face is bitter resilience.
And for what?
I have disagreed and gone away . . .

## 1 Corinthians 13:11

"When I was a child, I spoke like a child, I
thought like a child, I reasoned like a child.
When I became a man, I gave up childish
ways."

One Spirit,
one wind,
one breath
led us each by the hand
passed the door of death,
down the hallway on the left.

Light burst behind the shape.
Don't turn yet; don't turn.
Work down the hall and to the right
until all of you is paper.
Then come: burn with us.

## Numbers 22:22–33

"But God's anger was kindled because he
went, and the angel of the Lord took his stand
in the way as his adversary. Now he was riding
on the donkey, and his two servants were with
him. And the donkey saw the angel of the
Lord standing in the road, with a drawn sword
in his hand. And the donkey turned aside
out of the road and went into the field. And
Balaam struck the donkey, to turn her into the
road."

Seer could not see;
no eyes has seen
or ear has heard.
He has spoken a word . . . yes,
But here we are, mute and deaf.

The rod-beaten donkey,
well-deep eyes,
was not surprised,
but the blind man was.
The gauze of sense
wraps around the head,
so that we feel alive
when inside we're dead.

### *Romans 5:9*

> "Since, therefore, we have now been justified
> by his blood, much more shall we be saved by
> him from the wrath of God."

It came upon our blackness,
cold and thick;
our hearts turned.

Drip by drip our opaque
became translucent.
We had a new wish for union,
blooming like a white rose
in the early morning.

Blood is so black
it turns the black away,
for even the darkness
does as He will say.

## Psalm 13:3

"Consider and answer me, O Lord my God;
light up my eyes, lest I sleep the sleep of
death."

When my eyes are closed,
Satan comes in through a window.
He cuts up my memories,
quilts them together,
and rolls them in the dirt.

When I awake in you, I know my nakedness;
my eyes set right: the window was closed.
And I was scared because I supposed
I was alone in my blindness,
but you candle your way into my black,
telling me how to see
by showing me how to hear.

### Mark 1;9-12

"In those days Jesus came from Nazareth
of Galilee and was baptized by John in the
Jordan. And when he came up out of the
water, immediately he saw the heavens being
torn open and the Spirit descending on him
like a dove. And a voice came from heaven,
'You are my beloved Son; with you I am well
pleased.'"

He came out dripping,
steeped in Spirit,
so much so that John could hear it:
every drip a word dropped
loud as thunder from the clouds.
And his wool-soaked clothing,
heavy with resurrection,
spoke also of a holy river
from a holy God
and a holy giver.

### *The Seine of God (Mark 1:16)*

> "Passing alongside the Sea of Galilee, he saw
> Simon and Andrew the brother of Simon
> casting a net into the sea, for they were
> fishermen."

God is a great seine,
drifting in the deep,
holding fish at tiny intersections
of providence, grace, mercy, and love.
These are his knots.

But he is no fisherman's trap;
he just wants to hold, to embrace.
But fish are bold and foolish.
Seeing a mirage of freedom
in the open waters, we fin our way out,
leaving the net wanting:
an idea we will never understand.

## Romans 8:5

> "For those who live according to the flesh set
> their minds on the things of the flesh, but
> those who live according to the Spirit set their
> minds on the things of the Spirit."

"Home," he said to the window,
and he did not look to us.
The dust of our emotion
turned the air yellow.
Only one want
fluttered around his bedside
like a hummingbird.

## *Transfiguration*

Up the mountain went their little legs,
leather stamping stone.
Who would have known
the joyful dread in those legs
as they came back down,
leather beneath bone:
the animal hide and the earth
applauding a grand
conversation.

### *The Origin of Night*

It was a slow turning
of the black pages of beginning.
Breaking like waves on a shore
were God's soft words to himself:
a conversation fit for a living room.

"Let there be…" and then
a long pause while the Trinity communed,
huddled around the idea like elephants
circling a water hole,
speaking as if to introduce an old friend:
"light."

It was only then than night crept out as a boy
from the bushes, too shy to speak,
a smile saying, "Use me, too."

### Genesis 2:8

> "And the Lord God planted a garden in Eden,
> in the east, and there he put the man whom he
> had formed."

The gardens I tend are gardens of words,
rose-red verbs among green-grass nouns,
but attached (root, stem, and thorn)
to earthen sentences still damp
from a morning's meaning.

Nouns are the leaves of weeds and wild herbs;
crush one in your fingers,
and an ancient scent overwhelms.

Prepositions run the base of the root system,
tying bold, white threads to happy dirt.
I weed out the unnecessary noun phrases,
and leave a small measure of redundancy.

So all grows without my hand to guide it,
but God is happy when his creatures join him
in the commune of speech,
even if only by carelessly brushing
the outer wall of plants with their ankles.
Maybe the dew from the morning will awaken
them.

## *Genesis 5:5*

> "Thus all the days that Adam lived were 930
> years, and he died."

Must have been strange
when the first one died.
Children around a body:
trees around a dry creek bed.
What had happened?

As when my father died
and one less was felt.
Here we only like addition.
Still, Seth would have been in straights:
what and why,
what and why
is this stopping?

Our questions are heartbeats.

### Daniel 4:33–34

"Immediately the word was fulfilled against
Nebuchadnezzar. He was driven from among
men and ate grass like an ox, and his body
was wet with the dew of heaven till his hair
grew as long as eagles' feathers, and his nails
were like birds' claws. At the end of the days I,
Nebuchadnezzar, lifted my eyes to heaven, and
my reason returned to me, and I blessed the
Most High, and praised and honored him who
lives forever."

No sweat ever glistened this way;
soft on the forehead it lay
and fell to the ground: a salty crown
for a king who had long been away.

### Matthew 5:42

> "Give to the one who begs from you, and do
> not refuse the one who would borrow from
> you."

Such is the heart of God:
open wide like a tree
licked by lightning,
the pith raw and gold,
veined and grained,
weeping out sap in the open air,
ripe in the sun.

### *John 14:5*

> "Thomas said to him, 'Lord, we do not know
> where you are going. How can we know the
> way?'"

Thomas, like you, I don't know what to say.
How can a man be a way?
Is his body a bridge?
Is his soul a sentence
I speak to unlock the gate to freedom
and remembrance?

### *Exodus 34:29*

> "When Moses came down from Mount Sinai,
> with the two tablets of the testimony in his
> hand as he came down from the mountain,
> Moses did not know that the skin of his face
> shone because he had been talking with God."

No, I would imagine,
he would not know his face was glowing,
skin heavy with light,
cheeks pinked and forehead beaming.
From mountain top to tent of meeting,
he could go no place where God's holy speech
would fail to pump his heart,
beat upon beat upon beat:
a holy life-blood that goes
even deeper than the earth.

## John 11:41 (Lazarus's Tomb)

> "So they took away the stone. And Jesus lifted
> up his eyes and said, 'Father, I thank you that
> you have heard me.'"

It was the smell she was afraid of,
the must from the must of death.
Her brother was now beyond loving,
his glory wrapped about him
in a dull blanket stained with spice.
She knew that men on that side of the stone
rotted to the bone, let alone
to the dark elements and the hallow dirt.

And yet,
what if decay
didn't win the day?
What if death
was not the last breath?
What if resurrection
emerged from the darkness
in the cave of her soul's doubt?

POEMS FROM THEOLOGICAL WORKS

## *Truth*

Truth is a person we join by preposition:
*in* is where we dwell,
not a stagnant proposition
or empirical spell.

Truth is God's speech:
Father by Son through Spirit.
Deafness is breeched
for those who hear it.

Truth is not alone;
it lives in community.
speech and thought, flesh and bone,
bear the mark of Trinity.

### The Giver (1)

Ancient, great, and evergreen,
God gives himself away.
And we receive him now unseen
with every dawning day.

The Son is true and real and good.
The Father always gives
so that we give back, as we should,
the life that truly lives.

### The Giver (2)

Father, Son, and Spirit, each to each,
God is a Giver well beyond reach.
But he gave himself below
so that we might hold and know
the truth that giving lends
ourselves to others' ends,
and calls us to adore
the God who gives much more
than we could ever seek.

### *Identity*

God of glory, grass, and men,
of colored things and spirits living,
tell me who I am again.
"A man among the God of giving."

Father, Son, and Holy Ghost,
speaking, sharing, giving chase,
you make me more; you make me most.
You paint into my penciled face.

In you, I am, my vine and door.
You grow me strong and call me in.
Whether I want less or more,
I find myself where you begin.

### *The Voice*

Ten thousand voices buzz like bees—
the sound and fury fill my ears.
But the ancient voice who walked on seas
always calls and guides and hears.
His speech is governing those bees
and asking every heart to listen.
Spirit, help me hear upon my knees,
and follow with the hope you christen.

### *The Presence*

I cannot see nor can I feel
everything I know is real.
God, your speech is here, with me.
There is no need for me to see.
I trust you here. I trust you there.
I trust you speaking everywhere.

### *He Said*

A silent God would never do,
not for Adam, and not for Eve.
We needed to be told what's true.
Only his words could bring reprieve.

And so God gave them—means to mirth.
Our life was tied to syllables.
God uttered, and we felt our worth;
his speech made us forgivable.

He spoke to tell us he was here,
amidst the trees, behind the sun.
And into every listening ear
he gave his word: he'd never run.

He would stay close, always present,
though we would cling to the great lie
that no king resides with peasants,
no God could live where men would die.

Still he continued, whispering strong;
even called out bodies from the grave.
But we didn't listen very long.
We'd need a greater Word to save.

And so God gave him, Son of man,
the Lord of heaven wrapped in earth,
light of light, the heart of his plan

to give us all a second birth.

God's presence spoken into flesh
to wave and walk and carry on,
a stalk of wheat that we would thresh,
a presence men would prey upon.

And so they preyed, and off he went,
right into Joseph's rocky tomb.
There in the dark God's presence lay,
wound in cloth and our own perfume.

But

A silent Word would never do,
not for Pilate, and not for Paul.
Through death the Word was uttered new,
resurrected speech for us all.

So do not ask for God to speak.
He's done that in our doubt and dread.
He speaks his presence to the weak.
We are alive because he said.

## The Haunting

I was a barn for God, broken, gray, and tired.
The horses and the hounds all left;
the owls and the swallows rest
their hollow bones on hay bale nests.
It seems my spirit has transpired.

The devil came as a farmer black.
He sent the animals away
and told no travelers to stay.
I couldn't keep the rain at bay,
and all I have is lack.

Then came a holy bird in me.
He perched upon my weakest beam,
told me it was time to dream
of horse and hen and hay bale steam,
of housing life resiliently.

"And as you shelter, never boast,"
he said from on the rafter.
"When you are strong hereafter,
and trade sorrow for laughter,
rehearse what matters most."

"You are no place for vaunting."
My tired frame just nodded,
as the old bird hopped and plodded,
singing of the home he spotted:

"I am here for haunting."

## A Prayer for All Apologies

God, you are the Finder.

In the deep and the dark,
where we can't see a spark,
you seek and you call,
breaking every weak wall,
and find your way in
through the sin.

Arguments and thoughts abound
for how to turn the lost to found.
But we have no control at all
over the lordly or the small
to force a vision of your face
amidst the chase.

The heart is such a fickle thing.
It dances to whatever sings.
Our world is bent on chasing voices,
Enslaved to all the other choices.
What can we do but point and pray
to the one who knows the way?

All lost are yours alone to find—
the sick, delirious, and blind.
Use our words and hands to frame
a window for your holy name,
so all the lost might pause to look

Inside your book.

We are the lost ones. Find us.
We are the hiders. Find us.
We are the blinded. Find us.
And help us find each other.

Amen.

### The Christ-Light

God lit a candle in your chest.
The wax is of the very best.
The wick is woven strong, unbreaking,
and the flame is of the Spirit's making.

### *The God of Light*

"The Father of lights"—that is your name,
a blinding brilliance among heavenly hosts,
for even angels with wings of flame
can't stare at Father, Son, and Holy Ghost.

### God of Golden Apples

A God of grace and golden apples,
a king of light and trees and flowers,
who makes the pollen dust his chapels
to fill with songs of daylight hours.

Your beauty is too great to gather.
As we rush through the pulsing wild,
ignoring all. Why would you rather
give us more than make us mild?

Pause the world. Let turning stop.
Halt rash feet and fumbling fingers.
Instead of deluge, give one drop,
and slow our hearts to let it linger.

### *Mystery beyond the Hills*

What mystery lies beyond the hills
before we came, before we stepped,
before we dressed in selfish wills
and clung to what cannot be kept?

That three are one, and gave and loved;
that holding harmony let off light;
that truth and beauty were not gloved,
but let us touch and hold them tight.

## *By Words*

By words we grasped a new pulsing heart,
casting the dead stone inside us away.
We burned with a flame only God could im-
part,
turning our shoulders from night into day.
Now speaking, communing, and growing to
one,
we eat divine words as morsels of light.
We feast on God's speech, the words of the
Son,
staring at him and eschewing the night.

### The Water Flows

The rivers ran, sweet, clear, and cold
as we swam near the God of light,
bound by a brightness, pure and bold,
that kept us from eternal night.

But we went off to chase a dream
of being gods ourselves, alone.
We built a dam to hold the stream,
to stay the Lord of flesh and bone.

But God would not sit idly by.
With one colossal surge of love
he sent himself, alone to die,
broke dams below with power above.

All waterways are open, friend.
The dams are cleared; the water's right.
We commune and stare, beyond our end,
as infant candles toward the light.

### The Circle

In a circle stood the souls of men,
ringing a light that glows and gives.
Our faces warmed; a soft amen
went out to the God who lives.

But we turned shoulders, showing backs.
The light we held went dark and bleak.
We wanted what we thought we lacked—
to be the great light others seek.

Yet the glowing, giving God pursued,
to turn our shoulders back around.
He sent himself to our great feud,
fit his feet for sandals, dropped a crown.

His giving of his blood and bone
put God's own light inside of us.
For there is one light, one love and throne
that we encircle with our trust.

Dark to light now, death to life,
we go low and give back the light
to other souls with wanting rife,
ready to lean out of the night.

### The Name

We once lived inside a voice
in a garden green and gold.
All we needed we were told.
We listened and we learned to hold
all hope and longing in a choice
to nod Amen and give God fame
as we were planted in one name.

But we were blinded by the chance
that we might be a voice alone.
We offered up our flesh and bone
to grasp at what we could not own,
and so began a restless dance
between old glory and new shame
as we left behind the ancient name.

A tower we thought we could build
to make our measure something seen,
a structure that would never lean
but mark us each as king and queen
so we could keep ourselves fulfilled.
But this was all a fragile game.
Our tongues were sundered by the name.

We wandered then and wander still,
across the hills, across the sea,
enslaved by what we thought was free
and groping for divinity,

as if we were not wholly ill,
and were not fading from the flame
that burns within the name.

Still with patient grace God spoke
and sang a savior into sight,
one from himself for men to fight
and bring us all into his light.
From deathly sleep we all awoke
and found a covering for our shame,
knit from that eternal name.

It should have been that all was lost
and scattered souls from hope depart,
but God gave his unending heart
to call us back from worlds apart.
And on a day called Pentecost,
the voice set flame to earthly blame
and called us home into the name.

Stone to stone and seam to seam,
the Spirit crafts and shapes and sands,
uniting strange and distant lands
into a frame marked in God's hands,
holes where holy love was dreamed.
God builds to show the world he came
And readies rooms within his name.

Made in the USA
Monee, IL
10 June 2023